My first look at

Mushrooms

Published by
Macmillan Children's Books
A division of
MACMILLAN PUBLISHERS LTD
Houndmills, Basingstoke, Hampshire, RG21 2XS
and London
Companies and representatives
throughout the world.

© First edition: De Ruiter, Gorinchem, The Netherlands

Printed in Italy.

British Library Cataloguing in Publication Data

Andel, Lydia van
My first look at mushrooms
1. Mushrooms
I. Title II. Sijl, Ineke van III. Agerbeek
Cherouke Ronkes IV Series
589. 2'223

ISBN 0-333-51757-1

Photographic Credits:

Jan van de Kam (p1, 2, 4, 5, 6, front cover)
Rein van Koppenhagen (p3, 7, 8, back cover)

My first look at
Mushrooms

MACMILLAN

1

toadshools

Look at the mushrooms. toadshools
They are growing in the wood.
Some have a short, thick stalk and
a fat, round cap.
Others have a long, thin stalk and
a thin, flat cap.

If you see mushrooms with red and
white spots, don't touch them.
They are poisonous.

Look carefully.
Can you see the stalk?
There is a ring around the stalk.
The ring show you where
the cap used to be.

Under the cap there are hundreds of gills.
Seeds called spores are between the gills.

3

The spores make these thin, white threads.
You can see how the threads spread
over the ground.
Lots of new mushrooms will begin to
grow from these threads.

4

Look at these mushrooms.
They don't grow in the wood.
They grow in fields and parks.
The spores look like ink as
they drip from the caps.
That's why these mushrooms
are called inkcaps!

These are mushrooms too.
They have brown and white caps.
These mushrooms are shaped like a fan.
But where are their stalks?

They don't have any because
they don't grow on the ground.
They are growing on a tree stump.
They grip the tree tightly, so they don't
fall to the ground.

6

Which animal do you think
has taken a bite out of the cap
and stalk of this mushroom?

Animals know which mushrooms are good to
eat but you don't.
That's why you should never eat
the mushrooms you find outside.

7

Here are some mushrooms that
you won't find outside.
They are grown inside in large trays.
You can eat these mushrooms.
They taste good.

When they are big enough they
are picked and packed into boxes.
Then they are sent to the shops
to be sold.

8

What's Dad cooking?

He bought the mushrooms from a shop.

They are safe to eat when
they are cooked.

Do you like eating mushrooms?

Don't forget - never pick wild mushrooms.

They could be poisonous.

Did you like this book?
There are lots more books for
you to read.

These are all the books in the
My first look at series:

 Spring

 Summer

 Autumn

 Winter

 Mushrooms

 Spiders

 A Butterfly

 Honeybees